MEMOIRS OF A WIDOW

By

ANA BLAIR

Memoirs Of A Widow

Ana Blair

Copyright © 2018 by Ana Aliceia Blair. All rights reserved. No part of this publication may be reproduced, stored in a retrieval system, or transmitted in any form by any means, electronically, mechanical, photo-copying, recording or otherwise without written permission of the copyright owner.

www.anablair.org

ISBN Book: 978-0-9974857-6-9
ISBN E: 978-0-9974857-9-0

Memoirs Of A Widow

Ana Blair

I Dedicate This Book In Loving Memory Of My Late Husband, Mr. Quinten James Blair. I Will And Have Always Loved You.

Memoirs Of A Widow

CONTENTS

Introduction 1
I Loved You So 4
My First True Love 5
Sun Kissed 6
When The Righteous Cry 8
Grace 12
Second Chance 13
No Longer Cut As Deep 14
Naysayers 15
A Dusted Sun 18
Finding Faith In A Struggle 20
Your Footprints 26
Become A Mother 27
A Part Of Me 28
The Silence That Screams 30
You Were God's Image In A Man 31
When Our Faith Moves Us 32
My World Stood Still 35
Putting Pieces Together 36
I Was Just A Woman 37
I Blow A Kiss 39
Tainted Love 40
Sirens 41
Acting On Faith 42
Memoirs of A Widow 45
We Will Always Be 46
So Soon 47

Moment	**48**
Today, A Friend Called	**50**
Blessings Through Obedience	**51**
Conclusion	**56**
Memories Through Images	**60**

INTRODUCTION

The first message that I delivered after the passing of my husband was one of hope. The scripture was 2nd Kings 4: 1-7; thus, reminding God's people that no matter how rough life's challenges may become, God will provide for us. The idea that the Holy Spirit would have guided me to this text is astonishing because I just experienced a similar situation. I gave birth to a son, and five days later my husband past away. So many thoughts swept my mind. I wondered: "Why?" I also wondered: "Am I going to be okay?" I asked myself: "What about my son?" A million questions seemed to come to my mind. It was likely that I could have related to the widow's circumstances in 2nd Kings. The topic of this sermon was: God Will Provide. I delivered this message through faith, and that is required for the believer because the Bible states: "The just shall live by faith" (Romans 1:17, King James Version). The

Bible also states that "Without faith, it is impossible to please him" (Hebrews 11:6).

To any believer desiring to please God, faith is essential to your walk with Christ because there will be moments when you do not know what the outcome may be. During these moments of uncertainty, you have to believe in your walk with God enough to keep moving forward. There will also be moments in your life when you may not understand God's plan for you, or you do not agree with His plans for you; however, prayer through faith will enable you to move forward in God's will.

Whenever I am faced with unwanted circumstances, I refer back to the text when Jesus prayed in the garden of Gethsemane. He prayed: "Father, take this cup away from me…nevertheless not my will but thine be done" (Luke 22:42). During my circumstances of giving birth, and then immediately memorializing my husband, I felt violated. I felt that God was absent from me or perhaps had betrayed me. These feelings of violations left me not only questioning God but also feeling angry with God. Here I am, wondering how could I have served God for so many years, and He allowed such tragedy to have happened. I also wondered about God's decision to allow my husband to transition and why so suddenly after I gave birth to our son. I wondered: "Why did he pass away during the time I gave birth?" Yes, I had many questions. Over time, I settled my thoughts and apologized to the monotheistic God for questioning what he allowed to take place. I apologized because I am only human.

My perception changed, and I began to thank God for the many memories I shared with my husband instead of feeling robbed or deprived.

During this season, my attention was brought to the woman who became a widow. The story introduces her not by her name, but by her faith which enabled a miracle to take place while she was in tribulation. Through faith, she pleased God, and her household became blessed. Through this book, you will find poetic expressions and analyzations of 2nd Kings 4:1-7. I pray that the stories shared will bless you, equip you to endure your storm, and draw you closer to Christ.

I Loved You So

The Father's ways, I will never truly understand.

You were such a loving and hard- working man.

Somedays we laughed as hard as we can.

Whenever we argued, we tried putting the pieces together again.

You were not only the love of my life but also my closest friend.

The day I last saw you, I never thought I would not see you again.

Our life was thriving with plans,

And raising Bryson from a boy to a man.

Somehow, I woke up and you were gone;

No final hugs or kisses and I was left alone.

I cried so many tears,

But none could bring you back here.

Just know that I loved you yesterday, today and will forever more…

I will teach our son how you loved him so-

Whenever I feel most broken,

I will hold to the love you gave and I will never let go…

Ana Blair

MY FIRST TRUE LOVE

My first love,

My true love,

The only one to make me smile,

And the only one to make me cry,

I have been missing you.

I wanted to call

To hear you say hi,

To hear you say bye,

Or ask: "Baby how was your day?"

This world was never your home.

Tell heaven I'm coming too.

As soon as I can get my house in order,

I will be as free as you

In a land where we won't grow old,

And where the half has never been told.

Sun Kissed

I was kissed by the sun, and embraced by God the day you entered my life!

Some of my fondest memories will always be knowing you as your wife.

In moments when the heart feels emptiest, I know that I will feel you in the wind.

Although I cannot hold you, I see you in nature, my friend.

You always said to me: "The day bricks fall out of the sky

Is when you will stop loving me!"

Because of death, you departed without saying goodbye

I grieved; So many tears I cried.

However, I am lifted because I have faith

That I'll see you again on that great day

When the saints will be gathered

To rejoice in heaven forever.

Sun Kissed (continued)

I can only imagine what it will be like above in God's sky,

But for now, I will send my love in moments passing by.

I pray you have had your time to talk to the Father.

Tell him while we weren't perfect, we always strived for better.

Tell the Master I said:

"I was kissed by the sun and embraced by God the day you entered my life!

Some of my fondest memories will always be knowing you as your wife!

I am going to need another touch of his grace

To get through this challenging stage."

Today, I often tell myself what you often told me

I often tell myself:

"When bricks fall out of the sky

That's when I'll stop loving you!"

I will love you my love all of life

Even until eternity

Because our love is till infinity.

WHEN THE RIGHTEOUS CRY

After the passing of my husband, I remember reflecting on what I do have. I recall evaluating my life and asking myself in so many words: "What are my lemons if I am going to create lemonade?" "What are my broken pieces if I am sailing in the storm on broken pieces?" I questioned myself ongoing about what opportunities I had to move forward. I did not want to become immovable from depression. I not only desired to grieve, and heal appropriately, but also I deviated my attention towards survival.

Although I was in pain, I had a son to consider. I knew my strength was not only for me but also for him. In connection with the scripture, in verse four, the pain was inflicted upon a servant woman who feared the Lord.

Even as children of God, we may not always understand why tragedy happens; however, if we focus on what we can do and on what we do have, it gives us hope. In Kings 4:2, after the prophet Elisha asks the widow what she has, the widow said, "Thine handmaid hath not anything in the house, save a pot of oil." This suggests that even though she was financially poor, she knew how to make the best of everything that she had.

When in pain, it is more critical than ever to make the best of what we do have instead of allowing what we do not have to worsen the pain even more. Grief will paralyze us if we let it. That is why it is essential to rely on God more than ever to build strength to keep moving forward. There are many ways to grieve; however, some are more constructive than others. For example, donating or volunteering at an organization that is dedicated to researching or helping those with the same disease that our deceased loved one had is very constructive. It is also an excellent way to honor the memory of our deceased loved one.

Personally, I gained strength because I had the opportunity to educate students. My husband believed strongly in one having a good education, and he was proud the day I became an educator. I felt blessed daily to teach students, and I always gave my very best work while teaching. I felt the need to do so in my husband's memory. Whenever I looked into the faces of my third graders, I saw my husband. I knew I was blessed with the opportunity to change their lives, and that connection strengthened me.

Whenever we consider grieving, there is no wrong or right way to grieve. We all will encounter different emotions, but similar feelings. However, we should believe the promises of God while we are mourning; this promise gives us an immeasurable amount of hope that surpasses all understanding.

No matter what is happening in our lives, God wants us to remain constructive. It is not about denying the pain. It is about using that pain to move forward positively. Is not that also what our deceased loved one would have wanted us to do as well? I am not suggesting that we should keep ourselves busy every minute. I believe that our deceased loved one has already fulfilled God's purpose for their lives. Now it is up to us to use the rest of our own lives to continue to live out God's purpose for us. Indeed, there is a purpose for each of our lives.

Pain may not necessarily be one of our desires for our lives, but it does come with the territory of living in this world. I wish I could have guaranteed that one will live to be utterly free of loss, pain, and sorrow of any sort. But that is not how this world works. We all know that this world is full of good and evil. Loss, sacrifice, and sorrow in some form are inevitable. Whenever we experience loss, we are often tempted to question or even dismiss God's existence altogether. But it is when we suffer a painful loss, it is more critical than ever to reach out to God. We need to reach out and to ask God what he wants us to do next and obey his guidance. During my greatest storm; the period in life in which I felt most vulnerable and defeated, I made only one commitment, and that was to fall to my knees to pray as frequent as possible. Although I was not able to reach out to Jesus Christ physically, I could have committed to pray one, two, or three times a day; however, I determined it to be necessary to pray as often as needed. I knew I needed God spiritually every moment.

God's guidance may not always come in the way that we expect. That is why we often miss it convincing ourselves that God is not answering our prayers. When my husband passed on, I was feeling the worst pain of my life. I was confused as to what I would do next. But I am here now because, like the widow in 2nd Kings, I did not give up on God nor his will for my life.

Just as loss or pain knows no boundaries, God's love has no limits. It is not the form or the details about the situation that matters most. Instead, it is how we use our faith in God in handling the case that does matter. One of the reasons that the Bible is so essential to our lives is because it contains passages to guide is through any situation that may occur. There is a whole book dedicated to handling pain, and that's the Book of Job. Job was a righteous servant of God. He righteously remained loyal to God in spite of his skin being leprous, not being able to move very much, and his friends refusing to understand his situation. As a result, when the Devil left Job, Job was rewarded with twice of everything that he had had before (Job 42:10). Grief and pain do make us stronger whenever we work through it.

2nd Kings does not go into a lot of detail as to what happened within the widow's life in chapter 4 after she sold her oil. But it does imply that she was able to pay off her debt and keep her sons. The blessings that came from her obedience is demonstrated in verses five through six when it mentions the oil miraculously flowing and filling the original jar until all of her borrowed jars were full. The widow's overflow of oil occurred because of her righteousness in obeying the Lord by following the Prophet Elisha's instructions.

One can conclude based on this text, that even during moments of the death or loss of our loved ones, God may speak to us and guide our lives. Whenever God speaks, let us be up doing. It is the action of our faith that prevents us from becoming stuck in the pain of the circumstance. It is the action of our belief that allows our situation to get better.

GRACE

You can't mimic grace.

It's not rehearsed on a stage,

And you can't mimic God's ways

To determine the unknown

Because you do not think as he does.

Caution; He's God of the universe!

His love heals the hurt.

Caution; He's God of the universe.

Second Chance

The reason lovers romance,

The God of a second chance,

The one who holds the world in orbit,

The one who spoke into existence all things bit by bit,

The one who moved majestically into time,

And before questions arrived, he answered the thoughts of the human's mind,

It is he who is monotheistic in his sovereign reign!

He reaches deep to heal the hearts of men.

His love heals the hurt.

He is God of the universe.

NO LONGER CUT AS DEEP

Swords that once cut so deeply

No longer cut as deep.

Obstacles that once caused pain

No longer feel the same.

I have learned to feel joy instead of life's misery

Because I grew from moments of defeat.

The deeper the pain felt, the stronger I became;

The stronger I grew, the better I am.

In the end, the pain developed me.

Know that the circumstance hurt me;

However, I am a child of the King.

Rather it was good or bad; I grew from everything.

There is a victory in my moments of defeat.

There is joy in my circumstance.

I learned to dance in the rain.

No. The circumstance did not defeat me

Because I believe in destiny.

During moments of life's darkness, light gravitates to me

Rescuing me from misery.

I see clearly because God's word is light unto my path.

During my darkest moments, God's love gravitated towards me.

Ana Blair

NAYSAYERS

Who am I to be the subject?

Why is my name in their mouth?

Should I feel pain or regret?

It is me they are talking about.

They were going to talk anyway

If I was with or without,

So let their words fall

Like mist around stars.

I shine through the fog even from afar

Because that's how stars are.

It would have been nice to have no haters

It would have been pleasant to have no naysayers

But life is not a fairytale

In your storm, some folks still don't want you to sail.

I would have liked for everyone to love one hundred percent,

But that is not how the story ends.

Therefore, instead of being afraid

I have freed myself from their hate.

I have lifted my head

Unto myself I have said:

"So be it if it does. So be it if it doesn't

Unto yourself be true

Because there is always going to be one or two

Naysayers (continued)

Maybe a few who will never truly love you.

You will win

If you love yourself time and time again!"

Looking back, I remember

I had some choices to make

Because life came at me so hard.

But I understood grace.

In the storm, I had to stay spiritually awake God enlightened me.

I fought and saw myself to a higher destiny.

Now I know

God is the captain of my sea.

The Lord and I will choose what is best for me.

Whenever the naysayers talk crucially,

I will not let their words affect me.

Because I have lifted my head

Unto myself I have said:

 "So be it if it does; so be it if it doesn't

Unto yourself be true

Because there is always going to be one or two

Maybe a few who will never truly love you.

You will win

If you love yourself time and time again!"

Naysayers (continued)

Let them talk, talk, talk

I'm going to walk, walk, walk

Let them in discord sew, sew, sew

I'm going to grow, grow, grow

Because I refuse

To lose.

That's the tenacity

That lifted me to a higher destiny.

Courage it takes

In your storm, you must fight and stay awake.

After a while, the rain will stop falling down,

And the naysayers will no longer be around.

A Dusted Sun

Orange highlights over a darkened sky,

Above the silence, I hear the voice of my son cry.

I have been embodied with strength for so long.

I ask myself: "Is this be the point where I go wrong?"

I feel pain from my left to right.

I missed sleep during the night.

I say to myself: "Put up a fight

And soon you will be through the night."

I missed my mama; she was my second mom, my grandma.

I never grieved the fact that my grandmother was deceased

Because I wanted to protect the son who was in my belly.

When he was born, I could not celebrate for his birth

Because of his father deceased and I was hurt.

"Breath in and breath out

You will win, no doubt" Is what I told myself longingly.

For once, I looked at the sun, and it seems dusted.

For once, I looked at my jewels, and they look rusted.

For once, a life that was so promising seemed only temporary.

For once, I looked up and no longer saw the Heaven God promised me.

I only see a darkened sky and a dusted sun.

I questioned God quietly: "Was this pain predestined since our lives begun?"

A Dusted Sun- (Continued)

Then I explained to him

How much I no longer understand…

I have always been optimistic

Even when the worst was realistic,

But tonight I feel the pain that starts from the gut.

These pains add to the invisible scars the heart.

For once, I looked at the sun, and it seems dusted.

For once, I looked at my jewels, and they look rusted.

For once, a life that was so promising seemed only temporary.

For once, I looked up and no longer saw the heaven God promised me.

Hope; hope; hope; I pray for hope for me.

Peace; peace; peace; I pray for peace for me.

Joy; joy; joy; I pray joy for me.

Love; love; love; I pray love for me.

For once, I looked at the sun, and it seems dusted.

For once, I looked at my jewels, and they look rusted.

For once, a life that was so promising seemed only temporary.

For once, I looked up and no longer saw the heaven God promised me.

FINDING FAITH IN A STRUGGLE

During certain moments, I experienced shock. I could be doing something such as holding my son in my arms or sorting through his newborn clothes, and suddenly became traumatized again. I realized during these moments that my emotions were still transpiring; thus, feeling whole again would not happen overnight. It would take days to become weeks, weeks to become months and months to become years for me to be completely whole. I accepted my brokenness. I accepted feeling in shock.

I also acknowledged that I needed patience with myself as I healed.

Before being a widow, I moved with haste at doing everything. Thus, I moved quickly. I had goals to accomplish, and I was in a hurry. Because of me acting with haste, I may have made mistakes. I did not learn the importance of patience even with myself until these circumstances arrived in my life.

I could not have rushed my healing. Because I could not have rushed my healing, I learned how to be patient. After my husband passed, I stayed with his family for several weeks. Being in the home where he grew up in, and around his loved ones brought me strength from him. I wanted to hold my son in the house that his father and I once called our parents' home. Even as an infant, I tried to familiarize my son with his family as I knew he we would need to be a part of their lives.

I remember holding my son for hours. I held him in my arms and placed his head on my chest. Holding him, and seeing his father's eyes through him brought me so much courage. I could feel my husband's presence, and I knew he would have wanted me to return to our home, and prepare a life for our son and I. Because I knew what my husband would have desired, I returned to my house and built a structured lifestyle.

Again, alongside these transitions, patience with myself and my situation was required of me. I remember being too traumatized to care for my infant child alone. I was blessed because our family took care of my son as I returned to work, church and adjusting to my new norm. Because I felt devastated, taking care of my son full time and building a career would have been impossible. I think it is critical for widows to understand that we all need support. If you do not have a support system, God would place people around you to help you. Yes, to help you. Mothers need help, and I needed help being a new mother and a widow.

I strategized types of help I would accept. Firstly, no one wants to lose a spouse. Secondly, no one wants to lose a spouse immediately after giving birth to their first child. I dealt with feeling torn apart. Normally, I would have tried to not ask for help, and make an effort to maintain my lifestyle alone. However, I came to terms accepting the fact that I am not "superwoman." I wish I could have been great or perfect by dotting every I, and cross every T. That was not the case. I came to the acceptance that I was not perfect. I came to an understanding that I needed help. I needed immediate help. The question I asked was: "Who is going to help me?" "What do I specifically need help with?" "How long will I need assistance?" I had many questions, and each one needed to be answered.

Within six weeks of my husband's passing, I made a commitment to myself that I would not become a financial burden to my parents or his parents. Yes, I knew that the support was there if I needed, but I wanted to provide for my son. In life, we should use things and love people, but some people do the opposite. They love things and use people. Considering the fact that I loved my family, and wanted to make wise decisions, I immediately knew that I was not going to behave selfishly or lack effort to strive for the best. I had work to do! I considered all of the things I would eventually need to pay for such as doctor visits, 1st birthday celebration, my son's education school, and the list goes on; I knew had work to do!

Because I had lost so much weight, the first step of action that I took towards my decision to work is that I went shopping. I went shopping and bought clothes my size. I stayed with our family for weeks and had very little clothes my size. The second thing I did was called my boss and told her I was returning to work, and to my home. Making this step after six weeks was paramount to my wholeness and well-being because if I had failed to pursue living again, I may have gotten stuck in the dark period that I was experiencing.

I had so much paperwork to complete that was in my mailbox. My home did not feel the same. Although my house was quiet home, it was still my home. After carefully thinking, I decided that the help I would have utilized would be for my son. I would allow the family to help me while I created ritual, routines, and structure. Over the next weeks, I began dealing with the financial side of my circumstance. I dealt with my husband's affairs alongside affairs that he and I had together. I prayed a lot during this time and connected with God. I am so grateful that God was there with me, and he took care of me.

Finances can be rough, and even dealing with family or people we love, it is impotent to the development of our relationships with them that we regard our finances carefully. You may ask me: "What do I mean?" Be careful what you borrow! Be careful not to borrow!

The Bible teaches: "Owe no man anything, but to love one another, for he that loveth another hath fulfilled the law." Romans 13:9. Another supporting scripture is: "The rich ruleth over the poor, and the borrower is a servant to the lender" Proverbs 22:7.

My husband and I often discussed Proverbs 22:7 together because he often explained to me that when people are in debt, they are as slaves to their debt. Whenever we are in debt, we are debtors to our lenders. Although I met my husband knowing little about finances, I loved listening to the many lessons he taught me. I remembered and embraced his teachings, and immediately after he passed, I enacted or behaved how I know that he would have desired.

Because my husband would have never wanted me to ask for financial assistance, I never did. My wants were last, and my needs were first. I knew our family was willing to care for my son, so I left him with family. I spent weeks sorting through piled up mail, closing affairs and becoming current on any bills I may have neglected due to my absence. I went to work with a smile because I was thankful for the opportunity to teach; the chance to be present and accounted for was a blessing.

Like the widow in 2nd Kings, I had choices to make, and I needed to make them quickly. Like the widow in 2nd Kings, my immediate reactions would have impacted the rest of my life. Like the widow in 2nd Kings, my response enacted with faith delivered me from possible financial distress.

During biblical times, whenever someone could not pay their debt, they often lost everything they had. The debtors were sold into slavery and thrown into debtors' prison as collateral. We may not have actual debtors' prisons today, but even debt can feel like a prison when we're thousands of dollars in debt, we can't afford to pay it back, and the creditors get on our backs. The current consequences for racking up debt are not as horrible as debtors' prison. However, high debt situations are always very stressful and can sometimes seem impossible to manage. That is where God comes in. With God, all things are possible.

If the widow's sons were taken to become slaves, the guards and prisoners would have treated her sons like livestock. Like any mother, the widow would not have wanted her sons to exist like that. She wanted them to live out their lives serving God the way that she and her husband did. She also knew that that is what her husband would have wanted as well.

Although debt is often very stressful, it also keeps us from taking things for granted. Debt is a constant reminder to us that "our" things are not ours. God creates everything, and that makes Him the true owner of everything.

In the case of the widow, it was her husband who created the debt. The fourth verse in 2nd Kings does not say whether the husband had a job or precisely what the family's situation was before he passed on. It only indicates that the widow was rich in thought in spite of being financially destitute. Being rich in view means maintaining faith in God no matter what. Inheriting a loved one's debt is challenging. It is also a challenge to go from two incomes to one income. Regardless of how the widow felt during this time, we know that she did not act in uncertainty. Through God's guidance, she became free debt and lived a peaceful life. We must believe in God enough to take action. With the Lord's wisdom and help, paying off debt is always possible.

Your Footprints

Thank you for leaving your footprints on the sands of my life.

Thank you for shining your love as light.

Thank you for always letting me see your point of view.

Thank you for loving me as much as I love you.

Because you I have known,

I have grown.

Your footprints will remain on my heart.

I will see you again one day when I too, will have a brand new start.

Until then, I will live in peace

And from prayers of comfort, I will never cease.

BECOME A MOTHER

If you would like to love differently, harder, and stronger,

If you want to experience agape love; the one that lasts until infinity

Give birth to a son or a daughter.

Go through the pains and even laughter.

Each experience deepens your heart a little more.

Soon the way you view love will be redefined.

Things I would not do for myself,

I do for my child.

Habits I would have never given up,

I have learned to let them go.

I never knew I would love him so.

I am a mother,

And before being a mother, I have never loved so deep it hurts.

In all things, I put someone else first.

His smile is the essence of my heartbeat,

And his life's journey is mine bitter-sweet.

If you want to love this deeply,

If you want love to sweep you off of your feet

Become a mother.

A Part Of Me

"Give him your heart; give him your soul.

Love him in a world that seems so cold,

And show him all the beauty life behold.

Beloved, love your lover wholeheartedly…"

Those are the words my grandmother said to me.

Those words completed me.

The day God called my husband home,

This was the task I was working on completing.

We worked to make our house a home.

Because death caused separation, I was left alone.

I had to stand still and pause

Because in moments life became a clause of what was.

If love ever happened to me in the same light again,

I know I've been blessed twice by God the son of man

Because he gave me my dream come true.

For moments, I was blessed to love the best man I knew.

A Part Of Me (continued)

Although he is no longer here

To let go has been my fear

Because I am the mother of his son,

A new life which begun.

My deceased love will always be a part of me.

I better understand the power of the Trinity.

I have experienced love as a threefold cord

Because there was I; there was he; there was God.

We planned for longevity

To love each other eternally.

Although he is not present physically,

He will always be a part of me.

THE SILENCE THAT SCREAMS

The silence screams your name

Since the moment you departed.

I no longer see life the same.

My beloved, I have been so brokenhearted.

You gave your heart to me,

And I in return vowed to love you beyond limits;

However, for a moment that wish was granted.

My love, you left so soon.

In sadness and grief, I felt consumed.

Death was my biggest fear,

And now my reality.

Is that the is no longer here

Whom I knew and loved me best.

You Were God's Image In A Man

You were God's image in a man.

You were crafted perfectly for me being your woman.

How I loved you!

I smiled at the smallest things you would do.

You crafted my life in abundance,

And where there were mistakes

We accepted that none of us were perfect

Although for each other we were heaven sent.

I know that I will smile again

Only if it is because of memories of you, my friend.

Your love is with me.

I feel it so heavenly.

Darling, I will never forget you.

Because of you, I exuded goodness, and I grew.

I will always remember you were God's image in a man

And you are crafted perfectly for me, your woman

WHEN OUR FAITH MOVES US

The story of the 2nd Kings widow is one example as to how our faith in God can motivate us to do things that seem unimaginable. In biblical times, prophets were often considered to be the only direct lines of communication with God. Today, however, we know that God communicates with all of us directly and continuously. The challenge we often encounter is that God's communication to us is not always in the form that we expect and we often miss His instructions because of it.

We also miss God's instructions because it often does not make sense to us at the moment that he gives it to us. For example, we may suddenly feel a powerful urge to go to a particular place, but we don't do it because it doesn't get any more specific than that. That is not how God works, though. God works by giving instructions one or two steps at a time. It is up to us as to whether or not we follow those steps.

In my experiences, I knew that I would be victorious. Thus, I knew that God would not leave me defeated. However, I did foresee the pain and devastations that I would endure in route to my destiny. I focused on taking one moment at a time. I knew that bit by bit; I would overcome pain.

The widow of 2nd Kings could have chosen not to follow God's instructions through Elisha. However, she would have put herself and her sons in great danger if she had not. The widow also did not allow any fears that she may have had to stop her from doing as God instructed. Like Job, she was rewarded with even more of what she already had. In her case, that was oil. The oil provided all that she needed to survive. The Bible does say that she was a prophet son's wife (Kings 4:1), but it does not provide additional details about the widow's neighborhood. One thing that is very clear, however, is that she had some very generous neighbors who probably either already knew her situation or were very sympathetic when she told them. As a late prophet's son's wife, she was probably also quite well-known in her community. As a result, she probably also wanted to maintain her example of faith for them as well.

The story of the widow in 2nd Kings is an example of the fact that it is not the how that is important. It is the maintenance of belief that God will provide no matter what. All we need to do is give our willingness, do our part out of love, and then everything will naturally work out well.

Our finite minds cannot see the bigger picture as God can. When we try to do things with a do-it-yourself attitude, we often put up a wall between ourselves and God. However, when we bring our God into what we are doing, we can achieve anything at all. Sometimes something is not meant to be done a certain way. Sometimes an individual task is not ours, but someone else's to complete, like King Solomon instead of King David building the Temple (1

Chronicles **22)**. King David had fought in so many wars and had not always been obedient to God. As a result, he could not build the Temple. But his son, Solomon, the wise king, could. That was because he had asked God to make him wise in every way. King Solomon, as a character, was a temple of God.

When we make ourselves temples of God, anything is possible. The widow in 2nd Kings may have been a prophet's son's wife. However, it was the way in which she willingly followed God's instructions that she made herself a true temple of God. She also did so in following her mother's instinct to do anything to keep her sons out of danger.

If there is one thing that God does not like, it is indecision (Revelation 3:16). By that, I mean doubt about our faith in Him. Being indecisive about what actions we should take is perfectly okay. Again, that is where God steps in. When He does, His guidance does not change. However, our finite human mind often gets in the way of it to the point at which we can't tell whether it is God's guidance or our wishful thinking. One thing that we need to remember is God's guidance may not always make sense at the time, and it may sometimes feel like it's more than we can handle. However, one thing that God never guides us to do is hurt ourselves or anyone else. So if you think that you are receiving "guidance" in that way, it is not God so do not follow it!

Whenever we take action, we always need to begin with the end in mind. It is still best to be considerate of what God wants rather than what we want. Once we make a decision, we are rewarded accordingly.

Ana Blair

My World Stood Still

I am not sure if ever all men will,

But there are times when the world stands still.

The night I touched your skin it was so cold.

I knew my life had taken a detour.

During the pregnancy of our son,

I had so many questions: "what if's and how come's?"

I remember even telling myself

If you were ever to leave us, that would be the worst.

Then I dreamed of seeing you aged at your best.

I dreamed of what life would be

As we placed our feet on the sands of time.

I knew I was yours, and you were mine.

Even when love flourishes like a vine,

And it's is heavenly and divine,

God still has a perfect will.

For me, that consisted of moments my world stood still.

What I know for sure is that I will see you again

I am confident in knowing that this is not the end.

Putting Pieces Together

I was trying to put pieces together from my yesterdays.

I was searching for hope my tomorrows,

But somewhere throughout the urgency to live

And the fear of not living at all again,

I felt a heartbeat inside of my soul,

And it has since made me whole.

I'm not where I want to be,

But I don't see life as a tragedy…

There was a heartbeat that grew inside of me

He makes me smile; he makes me smile

I am a singer of a different tune because of his smile

My son was given his father's name

I looked at him, and I love with a higher aim

My life will never be the same

The love he exudes is greater than any pain

A miracle for me;

My heartbeat till eternity

My son looks just like his father

He is memories of our love and laughter

My joy until infinity

My heartbeat till eternity

Ana Blair

I Was Just A Woman

I was just a woman; A woman who believed in destiny more than fate.

I was just a woman; A woman who believed in God more than Satan.

I was just a woman; A woman who loved her husband more than the world.

Yes, I was just a young woman; A woman who longed for kids and a family.

I was just a woman; A woman who was blessed to live her dream,

But suddenly life had me questioning:

"Why was destiny so cold? Could I have changed mine or his future?"

In my stormy sea

God's word reminded me:

Light never lost to darkness

Although death I could have never harnessed.

I Was Just A Woman (continued)

I understand that I am still a woman

Who is thankful to God for keeping me,

And even when he allowed pain

His grace was sufficient for me.

Yes, even in my stormy sea

Jesus spoke to me.

I cannot beat his giving.

My beloved now rests in the eternal land of the living.

Each day I am embraced

With God's unwavering grace.

Ana Blair

I Blow A Kiss

My fingers touch my lips,

And I blow a kiss to the heavens.

My fingers touch my lips,

And I blow a kiss to you.

Whenever I feel saddened,

I blow a kiss to the wind

Because I feel you in nature.

My lover and best friend,

Our hearts are twined forever.

TAINTED LOVE

Sometimes when love is tainted, it gives us the blues.

Sometimes tainted love makes us

Hate ourselves; however, we love whomever we choose.

Years, months and even days change a man or woman.

Sometimes we end up on the journey we never planned to embark upon.

We begin wishing peace and happiness from a heart of stone.

Everything that shines isn't gold,

But even new and shiny things become old.

In the journey of love, you never know

Who may become of the one you love so.

You have to keep love anew

Shine on and nurture the person who loves you.

Love is most beautiful when years past

Two find sparks and make the fire last

Tainted love is perfect

Because it is the closest to pure love that we'll ever get

Tainted hopes and tainted dreams

Tainted pain and imperfect love

Became the idea of perfection

And the keepsake of genuineness

Tainted love is love that is proven true

From the heart that beats just for you

Sirens

When the sounds of life siren no more,

When hopes and dreams have flattened

That you built and worked so hard for,

When your hands and feet are put to rest,

I pray the Master will allow you to rest

Knowing that you wrestled with the battles of this life,

But it was your best effort to live in the grace of his light.

No more sirens!

No more emergencies!

No more urgencies!

You are eternally free!

You are made whole eternally!

Memoirs Of A Widow

ACTING ON FAITH

Being a widow myself, I can't imagine how I would've felt if I had been left with one meager resource, and then instructed to borrow on top of it. However, as a mother myself, I can very easily understand that widow's wanting to save her sons from being sold into slavery above everything else. If slavery still existed for debtors, and I was in such situation, I would do anything to prevent my son from being sold. I know that my husband would have done the same to protect our son, and would have wanted me to as well.

Some other people in a situation like hers would be very hesitant to borrow for fear that it would increase the debt to be even more. In some cases, borrowing makes them feel ashamed. Some are too proud to ask for that kind of help. However, in the widow's situation, she practically couldn't afford to be ashamed or embarrassed because it was either her obeying the prophet, or give up her children to exist as numbers. Most importantly, she allowed her humbled faith and righteousness to move herself to do the right thing.

Similarly, Queen Esther did not allow even her fear of death to get in the way of her saving her people (Esther, 4:16, 5:1-3) from Haman's unjust plans to slaughter them just because her cousin, Mordecai refused to bow to him (Esther, 3:2). She let God move her to be brave and to do the right thing, even though it was illegal by Persian monarchy laws. Like the widow, Esther too was unexpectedly rewarded. In her case, it was by King Xerxes not only sparing her life but even going as far as to offer her half of the Persian kingdom (Esther, 5:3). Xerxes must have loved Esther very much if he so willingly spared her life like that. Back then, the king's queens and wives were often executed for just about any reason at all. Or maybe God was moving King Xerxes to spare Esther. Or perhaps some combination of both but only God knows.

When we are moved to do something that may not make sense to us at the moment, or that may even seem controversial for the greater good, we must not let even our fear of death stop us. After all, God did not put us here to serve ourselves and make our own lives comfortable 24/7. He placed us here to do His work. What God wants and what we want may not always be the same. Again, God can see the bigger picture of life; we can't. Doing the right thing is not defined by being belligerent and forceful. That's something that people still do all too often and what it leads to is being pushed even further back. Whenever we operate in the spirit of boastfulness, it is not God's way. Whenever we operate in arrogance, it is as if we put horse-blinders on ourselves. Those horse-blinders make miss seeing other options and even extraneous details that could be influencing what's happening to us. Like what the story of the 2nd Kings Widow shows, it means to carry out what God's work with a quiet humility and joyfulness. It also means having an attitude of gratitude in spite of any suffering that we may be going through at the moment.

I believe that an attitude of gratitude is what the widow in 2nd Kings likely had. If she'd had the opposite approach, she and her sons would have probably ended up dead as well. If not by slavery and filthy imprisonment, then by starvation. People who are not grateful are also more likely to believe that life is not worth living and give up. However, giving up doesn't please God at all. In fact, Proverbs 6:6-15 mentions the fact that people who are lazy will not be rewarded well. They're doing nothing only bring about their poverty and calamities.

Ana Blair

MEMOIRS OF A WIDOW

My love,

You were my friend.

In this life, I can count those on one hand.

I treasured you as God's favor to me your woman.

I remember the sweetest moments

Like the day we took pictures in the park,

Or sharing our meal until we both became full.

It was your smile; the little things that won my heart.

My love, my world has felt so cold.

I prayed your pain away

When you were challenged with life.

I prayed for your life and your soul.

You were like gravity

Which connected all of my broken pieces.

I have not known who to cry to

Because that person for me has always been you.

I have been missing you so!

These are the memoirs of your widow.

We Will Always Be

All I remember was holding your hand, and it felt so cold

Looking into your eyes and praying for your soul

But I know your heart was warmed

As you transition to your eternal home

You; my love, I will love eternally

You; my love impacted eternity

I will never forget you were God's gift to me

While I was with you, I loved you gracefully

I will always look for joy

In our son; our baby boy

I'll look for comfort in the promises that God gave us

That I'll souls will live after the flesh returns to dust

So Soon

It all happened so fast.

I lived in the present while pondering memories the past.

I was in sinking sand.

I needed you to hold my hand.

My world was still gloomy and filled with pain.

The one thing I desired was no longer mines

Because you were gone my love and sunshine.

Oh, how I longed for the taste of your lips,

And the touch of your hands.

You were God's man, and God sent you to me.

Your absence left me so empty.

May God bless our child

As I prepare to become

A mother to my son.

MOMENT

Lay the casket down;

Put in six feet in the ground.

Everyone is dressed in black,

And as I stare at the undertakers

I don't want to look back

Into the crowds of people

Because if anyone looks too deep

They'll see how lost I am.

If one stares into my eyes

They'll look into the face of misery.

As much as I love the Father,

I cannot deny my anger.

To question God, I should know better.

For a moment, I asked the Lord:

"Why me?"

Questions from the crowds are asked to me:

"Are you ok?

Are you goanna make it?"

I have been asked.

Truthfully,

I don't know if my strength is going to last.

It's hard moving into the future

Moment (continued)

When you buried the joys of your past,

And I don't want to be in remiss.

Excuse me if I hesitate

But I need a moment…

"Why me?"

I feel violated.

I want to be isolated

From the crowds,

And I do not want to make a scene and shout too loud.

As I look around, I see fathers, mothers and their child.

With tears, I look at the crowd and barely pretend to smile.

Troubles come to all

But for a moment, I felt so short of standing tall.

Moments of hope, I would steal

As I wonder…

Why me?

TODAY, A FRIEND CALLED

Today a friend called to check on me.

I felt blessed because someone cared for me.

She said:

"I have been where you are

Don't forget that you're God's star!

You can do anything as long as you first believe.

From this tragedy, you can even heal.

Keep your eyes on God's plan.

Keep your hands in the master plans.

He will lead you where you belong.

Yes, he will keep you strong!"

She continued to say:

"I'm going to pray for you

That you would find light and make it through.

To find comfort and move ahead!"

Oh, what joy and confidence I felt

All because of the words she said.

I became strong during a tragedy

Because a friend called to check on me.

Ana Blair

BLESSINGS THROUGH OBEDIENCE

The book of 2nd Kings Widows' story also demonstrates how much obedience to God's instructions is critical in leading to a gain of plenty. A prophet's instructions is like a doctor's prescriptions for life's challenges. When those prescriptions are followed, they lead to long-term prosperity.

Often, as in the scene with Jesus praying in the Garden of Gethsemane (Luke 22:42), what God wants us to do is usually the last thing in the world that we want to do. And yet, God never gives us more than we can handle as is necessary for our growth. For example, when my husband passed away, I didn't even know how I could manage my life or raising my son as a single parent. As you can imagine, I referred to the Garden of Gethsemane scene as well as the story of the widow in the 2nd Kings very often during that time.

I knew through the study of God's word that obedience was necessary and essential to my wholeness. There is a song that says: "If we trust and obey in God's word, he will make a way somehow!" These words can be a description of how I felt while I endured my storm. I only trusted in the Lord and leaned on his words. Again, it is when we are challenged in most painful times that it is essential to ask God what he wants us to do from there. It is even more critical that we obey that guidance even if it doesn't make sense to us at the moment, or if it's the last thing that we want to do. Because I was steadfast in my obedience to God, my grief for my husband eventually turned into the beautiful memories that I have of him.

Like Jesus not wanting to go through with the crucifixion during the Garden of Gethsemane scene, borrowing and selling oil was probably the last thing that the widow in 2nd Kings desired doing. However, by some miracle, the oil flowed and flowed until all of the jars were full (2 Kings 4:5-6). God's guidance can feel intimidating when it's something that we feel that we cannot do, or cannot handle at the moment. Again, we always need to remember that God never gives us more than we can handle.

It is also noticeable that the prophet Elisha instructed that widow to close the door behind her and her sons when they were about to pour the oil (2 Kings 4:4). This was probably because, first, they probably had no way of knowing exactly when the creditors would show up next. Secondly, thieves could have easily snatched it. The third reason was perhaps that they didn't want to risk a spark of gossip and controversy in their neighborhood in the way that Jesus' many miracles later did in entire towns and cities.

The prophet's instruction to close the door connects to our lives because like the widow and her sons, sometimes we must allow God to work in private. Yes, in private. People may be judgmental. People may be cruel. Even in controversy and adversity, some people will be supportive. However, I cannot express enough the importance of us knowing God, being patient with God and allowing him to work in private.

Our personal lives are not to be displayed before the world. Not everyone has to know everything that may go wrong or right with you. I remember getting up many mornings and crying as I prepared for work. I remembered the sirens that sounded so loud in my mind at the end of my workday when I became acquainted with silence again. However, I cried out to God and not to the crowds of people. I considered these moments in my life as moments of closing the door. I quietly coped with my feelings; thus, allowed me to heal. To any widow who may be broken, hurt and confused, I would advise you to do just as the scripture advised the widow, and close your door. Cry, grieve and mourn in private but be prepared for life when you open the door.

When it comes to privacy, the Bible also teaches us to pray in private. Jesus taught that when you want to pray, you should go into your room and close the door behind you. After all, prayer is one-on-one time with God and God can see everything that is done in both public and private (Matthew 6:6). If He can see that you're loyal to Him even in secret, you will be much rewarded. Like Jesus also said, God has no patience for shallowness. He doesn't like when people randomly pray aloud in public for the sake of keeping up the public image (Matthew 6:6). Although prayer is essential, it is only effective if done in the spirit of humility.

Miracles meant for the individual, such as the widow in 2nd Kings, are better off being done in private for the same reason that it's essential to keep prayer private. It is when we are alone that we are most vulnerable. When we obey God in our vulnerability, He greatly provides for us in one way or another.

Scripture:

"For we know that if our house of this tabernacle were dissolved, we have a building of God, a house not made with hands, eternal in the heavens.

For in this we groan, earnestly desiring to be clothed upon with our house which is from heaven:

If so be that being clothed, we shall not be found naked.

For we that are in this tabernacle do groan, being burdened: not for that we would be unclothed, but clothed upon, that mortality might be swallowed up of life.

Now he that wrought us for the selfsame thing is God, who also hath given unto us the earnest of the Spirit.

Therefore, we are always confident knowing that, whilst we are at home in the body, we are absent from the Lord.

(For we walk by faith, not by sight)

We are confident, I say, and willing rather be absent from the body is to be present with the Lord."

2ND CORINTHIANS 5: 1-8

CONCLUSION

In conclusion, final memories about my husband are that he had a warm smile, he was very hard work and most importantly we loved each other. I most enjoyed seeing him smile. Knowing that I made him smile also made me happy. He smiled when we went on dates. He smiled when I made his favorite meals. He smiled at the thought that we loved each other for so many years. He smiled because he was so happy on his wedding day, and he smiled at the idea of becoming a father.

During his repass, I walked outside. My great-grandmother who was ninety-two years old walked up to me. She touched my hand, and she said: "In the name of Jesus, you are going to make it. You will be strong!" Immediately, I regained strength and faith.

My great-grandmother also prayed for me as a child. She prayed for me to serve God, to meet a husband, and for he and I to become like two peas in a pod. I smiled at her prayer. During the time she met my deceased husband, she said to me: "I reckoned he is goanna be the one. You soon will cut cake." My grandmother spoke somewhat Gullah being a southerner of her age. This statement meant she felt my friend at that time would have eventually become my husband, and soon he and I will marry. She was correct.

More than anything other than how much I loved my husband, I loved the community and family who prayed for me during such a vulnerable time of transition. As Christians, we do not always trust God; however, we should trust God no matter what we experience. It is essential that we not give up on God in challenging times. When forsake God, we become even more discouraged.

There are various Biblical references which demonstrate the importance of one having an ongoing faith in God. For example, Joseph was very tempted to give up on God when his jealous half-brothers threw him into the dry well (Genesis 37:24). Joseph was sold into slavery instead (Genesis 37:28) partly because of his faith. We do know that Joseph made the best of out of every situation that he got into. He later became the Pharaoh's right hand (Genesis 41:40) because of his faith and obedience to God.

When his brothers later visited Egypt and Joseph revealed himself to them, he insisted that it was not them but God who had sent him to Egypt. If he had not foreseen the seven years of drought and averted the mass starvation of their people, a good portion of God's people would have all died out

(Genesis 45:5-8). Joseph's faith could also compare to that of the centurion whose servant Jesus later healed (Luke 7:1-10).

The centurion's faith was so great that all he needed was to hear Jesus say the word for his servant to be healed. Instead, it was the centurion's faith alone that healed the servant (Luke 7:1-10). The centurion's story is a demonstration of the fact that all we need to do is to trust God entirely to receive a miracle.

We should always trust God, even in the times of hardships. In fact, the not so good times are when it's the most essential to maintain an attitude of gratitude.

When my husband passed on just days after our son was born, to say that I was not prepared is an understatement. I was not expecting him to go so soon and was hoping that he would get to enjoy our time raising our son together. Today, I honor that God had other plans. Even though we may not be able to figure out what that reason is, we should always trust that God has not left or forsaken us.

When Jesus was suffering on the cross, even Jesus felt that God had forsaken him (Matthew 27:46), but He humbly gave up his whole being to God so that the last part of His mission would be fulfilled (Luke 24:46). I believe that it was because Jesus' great faith in God that genuinely made the resurrection possible. Jesus knew that he was meant to die by being crucified and then resurrected (Mark 8:31-38). In fact, he spoke of his death in that exact manner more than once as if he was meant to die in only that way and absolutely nothing could have prevented it. The Bible doesn't detail the tone in which Jesus used to say it, but since he said it more than once, it indicates that things could not have happened any other way. If it had, the people of that and future generations would not be able to live with any hope of having direct faith in God at all.

Trusting God is always the most important thing that us Christians can do. It is the foundation in which everything originates, is preserved for a time and then passes on. Not knowing the outcome can be scary. But we also need to remember that the result is partly a consequence based on our actions. If God did everything for us, it would be like a parent doing everything for a child. In those cases, the child doesn't have the room to grow and become independent. If God had not given us free will, there would be no point in us living.

We may face various trials and tribulations; however, the gift of life comes from God. We should be thankful to Him.

Memories of a father and a husband whom I will always treasure and love.

Mr. Quinten James Blair

Ana Blair

Memoirs Of A Widow

Ana Blair

Memoirs Of A Widow

Ana Blair

This Is Not The End

People have said to me: "The transition of death means life has come to an end."

I know them to be unwise

Because we live to live again…

And sometimes in life we have to learn

To love and live again

For if this was truly the end

It would only be reciprocal to begin again.

www.ingramcontent.com/pod-product-compliance
Lightning Source LLC
Chambersburg PA
CBHW070102100426
42743CB00012B/2639